KINGDOM LEAGUE INTERNATIONAL

Structures & Strategies

Kingdom League International

© Copyright 2015-2018 by Tim Taylor

ISBN-13: 978-1514673355

ISBN-10: 1514673355

Other Books by Tim Taylor

Developing Apostolic Strategy

Operation Rolling Thunder Revised Edition

Build the Wall

Published by:

4004 NE 4th Street, Suite 107-350, Renton, WA 98056

www.KingdomLeague.org

Introduction

Introduction

Just as there are natural seasons which cycle throughout a year, there are spiritual seasons as well. These are *kairos* times which are marked with a restoration of truth. With each restoration of truth God calls a people out who will pioneer and lay a foundation. These seasons are marked by apostolic people who choose to do what has not been done, to go where others have not gone, and to live the message they proclaim. This is the heart of a leader, and a reflection of one of the characteristics of an apostolic gift—an apostolic people.

There is a kingdom move underway inspired by an ancient pattern. It reflects a heavenly reality that we seek to model in a modern setting with people who will re-present the gospel of His kingdom like Jesus did; with power and character. God is calling forth the army of the Lord like Israel when they came out of Egypt, and like the dry bones which came together miraculously as breath came into them in Ezekiel 37. It is an exceedingly great army which functions as one body. God is calling forth a people who'll become the answer to Jesus' prayer, *"that they **all may be one**, as You, Father, are in Me, and I in You; that they **also may be one in Us**, that the world may believe you sent Me"* (John 17:21, NKJV, emphasis added).

Kingdom League International is a church as well as an association of churches, ministries, and ministers. We've been called out for such a time as this. Who is part of the league? People who represent every gift our heavenly Father gave in Romans 12, every gift Holy Spirit gave in 1 Corinthians 12, and every gift that Jesus gave in Ephesians 4:7-11. Every person fulfilling their God-given destiny is needed. Our passion is to see our Lord Jesus Christ glorified and to see His gospel of the kingdom presented in the power and character that He modeled for us at the start of the first century Church.

Founder, an apostle & presiding bishop

1

CHAPTER ONE

History

The founder of Kingdom League International, Tim Taylor served as a naval officer in Operation Desert Storm. While there he had an encounter with the Lord where he was shown what would come in the years ahead regarding:

- the restoration of David's Tabernacle,

- the mobilization of the army of the Lord,

- and the call to equip leaders with the principles of corporate strategic warfare.

Tim returned in 1991 and went on a ministry trip to Israel with his wife, Brenda. While on this trip, they were called together into the ministry. Through an amazing set of divinely orchestrated situations and relationships, Watchman Ministries

International, a 501(c)3, was commissioned and launched in 1992.

Beginning with a small congregation in Springfield, Oregon, Tim and Brenda began to act upon their revelation and prove God's word, ... and prove the word they did. Working with small teams of prophetic intercessors and with leaders from the media and city council, they saw their city pass the first pro-family legislation in the United States!

Captured by a vision for unity in the body of Christ, they were the first to mobilize churches in the greater Lane County area for the "March for Jesus." During the march, over a thousand Christians from a multitude of congregations representing many denominations joined them to celebrate, pray, and worship Jesus. The event was accompanied by several prophetic teams deployed throughout Eugene and Springfield, Oregon. The result of this joint operation led to real transformation. Because Christians mobilized strategically behind a unified purpose, Hemlock Society (the organization which headed up "right-to-die" issues and supported euthanasia legislation in the United States), left the state. Property values rose and their city won the Sony contract which led to 300 new jobs.

The positive outcomes only spurred them to seek applying the principles at a greater level. Over the next ten years Tim and Brenda served as mission directors, itinerant ministers, elders, leaders of short term mission trips, and in a host of other conferences and church-related events. Starting in 1999, Tim entered the corporate world where he used these same principles to help his company prosper while serving Fortune 100 companies. All the while, Tim and Brenda sought to apply the principles on a greater level. They had been captured by the vision of projecting power to enforce the will of King Jesus that resulted in the tangible transformation of a community.

At the end of 2002, Tim was called back into the church world full time. By 2003, they had their first opportunity to present their vision to church, business, and government leaders in Nassau, Bahamas. God gave them several supernatural signs that spurred them on until they developed and presented a strategic prayer mobilization plan in 2005, beginning in Washington State. It was called **Operation Rolling Thunder**. This simple, yet powerful plan empowered and connected people from Charismatic to Catholic and from Presbyterian to Pentecostals to establish 24/7 prayer while forming strategic councils in the 7 spheres of society: church, business, government, media, education, healthcare, and the family.

In 2008, Tim had a one and half hour encounter with the Lord where God revealed His desire and design for apostolic resource centers (ARCs) to be established in cities, while concurrently connecting to others. The revelation given to Tim in 1991 was a foundation from which this could build, highlighting the role of councils and the importance of covenant/league.

During 2008, Watchman Ministries International received five reports from leaders stating that city prayer centers were launched through their use of Operation Rolling Thunder. Light of the World Prayer Center was the first in Bellingham,

Washington and was followed by Mount Horeb Prayer Center in Hakalay, Myanmar (Burma). Two more were established in Pakistan, and one in Kenya.

The supernatural, repeatable results all pointed to real transformation. By 2011, leaders in over 36 nations had reported things such as:

SUPERNATURAL, REPEATABLE RESULTS ALL POINTED TO REAL TRANSFORMATION.

- 31 city prayer centers birthed,

- 40+ church plants,

- numerous examples of church growth,

- decreasing crime,

- droughts broken,

- abortion clinics closed,

- elections impacted,

- corruption in government exposed,

- miracles,

- healings,

- epidemics stopped,

- reconciliation,

- economies prospering,

- ... and much more!

All this was the result of a strategy that empowered churches to invite God's abiding presence in their community through strategic prayer and honoring jurisdictions.

Tim foresaw the coming persecution in America—the attack on the First Amendment, and on God's design for families. Apprehended by a vision of Christ's kingdom government for the Church, he spent the next two years researching Church history in the United States as well as the history of non-profits or 501(c)3s. After consulting with a constitutional attorney with an understanding of common law, Kingdom League International (KLI) was launched in 2011. It is not designated by the governement as a 501(c)3 charitable organization, but rather it functions as a church and an association of churches, ministries, and ministers.

We at KLI have uniquely positioned ourselves to empower the Church to stand and to give voice to the gospel of the kingdom of our Lord Jesus Christ in these troubling times. In a chapter to come we will address church government and what we can offer churches and ministers who seek an alternative to organizing as a non-profit corporation.

Arise, shine; for your light has come! And the glory of the Lord is risen upon you. For behold, the darkness shall cover the earth, and deep darkness the people; But the Lord will arise over you, and His glory will be seen upon you. The Gentiles shall come to your light, and kings to the brightness of your rising.

—ISAIAH 60:1-3 NKJV

2

Truths

The following concepts are based upon truths which have greatly impacted Tim and Brenda. The vision, missions, and values of KLI which follow are an expression of our desire to walk these truths out by putting our faith into action with wisdom, based upon love. These scriptures and concepts are a critical components of KLI's purpose.

RESTORATION OF DAVID'S TABERNACLE

Restoration of David's tabernacle is expressed through the administration of teams of people within a city to lift up continual prayer, praise, and worship. It also requires the formation of councils in all spheres of society which is a way of gathering the elders at the gates. (See Amos 9:11, Acts 15:16.)

- 24/7 prayer establishes the mountain of the Lord's house of prayer also referred to as for all nations over every other mountain in society. This is also referred to as Mount Zion. (See Isaiah 56:7, Isaiah 2:2 and Micah 4:12.)

- Continual prayer, praise, and worship seats in the courtroom of heaven so we can plead our case. (See Psalm 22:3, Micah 6:1, 1 Samuel 24:15 and Jeremiah 2:35.)

- Praise is a weapon to enforce the will of God. (See 1 Chronicles 16:7, Psalm 2, Psalm 110, Genesis 49:10, Psalm 60:7.)

To learn more visit KLI's web store for "The First and Second Kingdom Congress, The Apostle's Revelation of David's Tabernacle, Operation Rolling Thunder, and Keys to Transforming Your City & Region with Power."

BUILDING THE WALL OF PRAYER

Every reformer in the Bible was inspired by the pattern King David established on Mount Zion in the City of David. Building the wall of prayer is a critical component of that pattern and empowers the Church to:

- **Establish a watch and a stronghold in their city or region.** This is accomplished by building a wall of prayer and setting a watch like the one modeled by the reformer in Nehemiah 3-4. The City of David was a stronghold (2 Samuel 5:7) and was essential in providing a place for the administration of prayer, praise, and worship in the tabernacle of David.

- **Connect the church at large with house of prayer ministries.** Just as Nehemiah's wall served the complimentary and essential assignment Ezra had to restore worship in the temple in Jerusalem, the wall of prayer is to be connected to and integrated with houses of prayer.

- **Establish strategic operation centers that facilitate watching, praying, and the gathering of natural and spiritual intelligence for leaders.** The Hebraic word for city is *iyr.* This term means "a place guarded by a watch." In Nehemiah's time Hananiah, the captain of the citadel, would have administered the watch for the city. Historical documents show that the citadel was located next to the tabernacle of David and would have served as a strategic operations center for city leaders. We find that co-locating a strategic operations center with a ministry functioning as a house of prayer serves the community well.

To learn more visit KLI's web store for "Build the Wall."

MOBILIZING AND CONNECTING THE CHURCH

KLI is committed to mobilizing and connecting the Church as one body, and one army with different functions. Family by family, congregation by congregation, city by city, county by county, state by state, and beyond ... all united by one purpose. (See Ezekiel 37:1-10, Joel 2:1-11 and 1 Corinthians 12.)

- The responsibility of an army is to project power to enforce the will of the government it represents. In this case, the Church is responsible to project power to enforce the will of King Jesus. (See Matthew 6:10 and 1 John 3:8b.)

- Each person to is responsible to fulfill their God-given assignment in the context of their family and their congregation within the city they reside. (See Ephesians 4:11-16, Romans 12:1-9 and 1 Corinthians 12:4-14.)

- The Church is to be one even as Jesus and the Father are one. (See John 17:21 and Psalm 133.)

- Jesus gave us a government structure and the gifts to establish that structure, whose jurisdictional assignment and power come from heaven. (See Ephesians 2:19-20, Ephesians 4:7-11, 1 Corinthians 12:28, 1 Timothy 3:1-13 and Titus 1:5-16.)

- KLI is restoring the use of councils in the Church and in the 7 Spheres of Society (See Proverbs 24:3-6.)

To learn more visit KLI's web store for "Developing Apostolic Strategy, Strategic Leadership, The First and Second Kingdom Congress, The Apostle's Revelation of David's Tabernacle and The Apostolic Reformation."

... ALL UNITED
BY ONE
PURPOSE.

3

CHAPTER THREE

The Vision and Purpose of Kingdom League International

OUR VISION

Transform society by the presentation of the gospel of the kingdom of our Lord Jesus Christ through the Church.

NO VISION IS FULFILLED ALONE

No vision is ever fulfilled alone, and every vision is always tied to a bigger vision. KLI is a network of kingdom-minded ministers, ministries, and churches. We are a family of families who have been united by vision and stay connected through covenant. As each family grows, they become like a tribe with

WE PROJECT
POWER TO
ENFORCE
THE WILL OF
KING JESUS.

their own unique gifts, talents, callings, and ministry expressions. KLI helps unite these tribes and project power to enforce the will of King Jesus.

The vision, missions, values, and culture of KLI helps us and others discover where we fit. Our goal is to interconnect with other kingdom-minded leaders and ministries whose relationships and collaboration will help each of us fulfill our God-given destiny in Christ personally and corporately. This kingdom network, this spiritual army, this tribe of tribes needs to grow as large as our heavenly Father's purpose and destiny requires.

The way we like to build our network is to challenge the inquirer and ourselves to pray with Psalm 139:15-16 in mind and ask the Lord saying, "When You envisioned my life before I was ever formed, whose life did you envision me being entwined with for Your purpose and Your glory?" We take covenant relationships seriously, and expect God to speak to the inquirer as well as to us.

WHAT DOES THE NAME MEAN?

The very name "Kingdom League International" and the corresponding logo is not only the name of this church and network of churches and ministries. It is also an apostolic decree and a prophetic proclamation of our Lord's desire to have a kingdom of leaders in league with one another for God's glory and His purpose.

> Here is a link to a 10 minute online video which provides great insight: http://www.kingdomleague.org/vision--missions.html.

OUR MOTTO

We are all for one, King Jesus! And we are one for all, the Church, the Ekklesia, the called out ones.

KINGDOM

Through the years, God has given Tim and Brenda strategies which have proven to unite and connect many diverse churches and denominations. The key is focusing on our common passion to transform their community through **the presentation of the gospel of the kingdom of our Lord Jesus Christ**. We highlight where we are in agreement and unite behind a common purpose.

Jesus began His ministry presenting the gospel of the kingdom. The word "kingdom" identifies the objective and answers "What is our message?" In Revelation 1:6 and 5:10, we find that we are to serve as kings and priests to our God and Father, and we are to reign on this earth as Jesus did. This requires an understanding of a kingdom:

- responsibility,

- authority,

- jurisdictions,

- dominion,

- and the role of kings.

It requires that we understand to "rule and reign" begins first within our personal lives, and then extends to every area for which we have responsibility.

> *For the kingdom of God is not eating and drinking, but righteousness and peace and joy in the Holy Spirit.*
>
> ROMANS 14:17

> *Nor will they say, "See here!" or "See there!" For indeed, the kingdom of God is within you."*
>
> LUKE 17:21

> *From that time Jesus began to preach and to say, "Repent, for the kingdom of heaven is at hand."*
>
> MATTHEW 4:17

The Church is called to preach and demonstrate the gospel of the kingdom like Jesus did. When Jesus began His assignment, He was alone. He is the Chief Cornerstone of the Church. Whereas He began His ministry alone as the first and founding apostle, there are more than two billion Christians today. Until Jesus raised up disciples, there was no opportunity for there to be a larger corporate expression. Today the demographics of the world and God's Church are very different. There is much more to work with, and on a grander scale.

The administration, teamwork, and disciplines found in a kingdom are needed for a greater corporate expression to function. Our Lord foresaw this in John 17:21, when He prayed that we would be one even as He and the Father were one. Apostle James and the prophets foresaw this when they prophesied about the restoration of David's tabernacle. Therefore, KLI is drawing from the ancient pattern King David modeled as we seek wisdom as to how to mobilize the army of the Lord today—city by city—on behalf of the Lord of Hosts.

Jesus is King and is at the head of His kingdom. In Revelation 19:11, we see Jesus used to model the two primary functions of a king: kings make decisions (judge) and make war. A kingdom is a government. During his time in the Navy, Tim learned that armies exist to project power to enforce the will of the government they represent.

Ezekiel 37, and Joel 2, prophesied of the day when the Lord would have an army, a body that would come together as one. This is part of the purpose of KLI. It is to facilitate

ARMIES EXIST TO PROJECT POWER TO ENFORCE THE WILL OF THE GOVERNMENT THEY REPRESENT.

the mobilization of the army of the Lord; a spiritual army. Its purpose is:

- to war in the spirit against demonic forces that oppose our Lord,

- to see the veil that resides over people's hearts and minds lifted,

- and then to represent that gospel.

KLI is called to enforce the will of King Jesus on earth as it is in heaven.

So what is the gospel, what is that good news? It is that King Jesus is the way to salvation and our entrance into the kingdom. We don't have to be condemned to a wasted existence here nor in eternity. The Bible says:

And as Moses lifted up the serpent in the wilderness, even so must the Son of Man be lifted up, that whoever believes in Him should not perish but have eternal life. For God so loved the world that He gave His only begotten Son, that whoever believes in Him should not perish but have everlasting life. For God did not send His Son into the world to condemn the world, but that the world through Him might be saved.

JOHN 3:14-17

For He says: "In an acceptable time I have heard you, and in the day of salvation I have helped you."

Behold, now is the accepted time; behold, now is the day of salvation."

2 CORINTHIANS 6:2

We are called to go and make disciples who exercise their authority and make decisions like a king. This starts in our personal lives as we learn to apply God's word to our own lives and make changes. The good news is this: we do not have to stay the same. God's grace is available to help us, but is not activated until we make a decision to invite and accept God's enabling power—His grace.

Jesus provided us the pattern for Church government. When this pattern is combined with a study and revelation of the restoration of David's tabernacle and the role of councils, it provides insight as to how the Church can lay a foundation in a city or region that gathers the elders within the gates.

- It recognizes and honors jurisdictions.

- It positions righteous men and women to help discover what the Church ought to pray.

- In Psalm 68:11 it says that the Lord gave the word and great was the company of those who proclaimed it. In this same way, the Church is empowered to transform the spheres of society.

God showed Tim a system or a strategy which empowers the Church in a city to identify the fivefold gifts (apostles, prophets, evangelists, pastors, and teachers) God sent them while forming councils in each one of the seven spheres of society: church, business, government, media, education, healthcare, and the family. The Church council is further divided into councils that represent the fivefold giving us a total of 12 councils.

12 COUNCILS

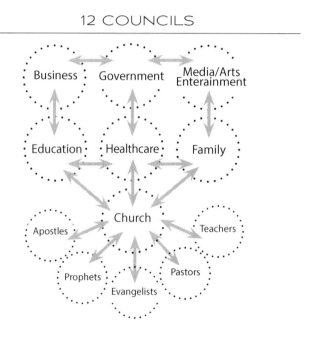

When we say "kingdom," envision not only the personal application of God's word in your life, but also its corporate application to the Church in a city and beyond. While we have personal authority, we choose as an act of our will, to filter each situation and decision through God's word so as to discover His will and wisdom as His ways are higher. Everyone associated with KLI works to put their faith in action with wisdom and the love of Christ so as to see Christ's kingdom established on earth as it is in heaven in every area for which they have responsibility.

4

CHAPTER FOUR

League

In Genesis 6, God speaks to Noah and tells him to build an ark. This is the first place in scripture the word "covenant" is used. *Strong's Concordance* says that this Hebrew word *beryith*, can also be translated *confederacy* or *league*. League is just another word for covenant. The use of the word league in society today sheds great insight into some of the concepts KLI is called to model.

The word "league" is a powerful concept. In modern usage it refers to groups or a federation of teams. In the kingdom league this addresses "who" is presenting the gospel of the kingdom and "how" we will demonstrate this message together. A league (or a covenant agreement) is essential to effective teamwork, mobilizing the army of the Lord, and connecting many different members as one body in Christ. The league serves as the ligament—holding the bones together.

Israel was one nation made up of 12 tribes scattered across different regions and cities. KLI is called to be like Israel: one nation with many tribes. The sports world provides even more great analogies for KLI. We are to be a team of teams.

Consider the National Football League (NFL). There are 32 teams in that league. The Seattle Seahawks are located in Washington, while the Miami Dolphins are located in Florida. Each team has the same positions, and signs a covenant agreeing to observe the same rules as teams in other cities. These rules and guidelines provide a basis that facilitates teams working and playing with one another. They are self-supporting, self-sustaining, and self-governing while at the same time they are interdependent. No team could exist alone much less thrive. Each team has also agreed to abide by the decisions of the league. The league is made up of three officers who, in a sense, form a council. They help arbitrate questions and challenges that arise between teams or with regard to league play.

Note, each team has its own unique identity, location, and organization. They have great latitude in the plays that are developed and how they run their organization. The league is the key that provides the ability for 32 different teams to play together.

Formed at the end of World Word 1, the League of Nations is another example. At its zenith it consisted of 58 members whose principal mission was, as stated in its covenant, "to prevent war and settle international disputes." It ended in 1946. The desire and goal to maintain peace was the goal that united them, but it was the covenant or league that empowered them to stay connected and actually enable diverse nations made up of different cultures to work together for a common purpose.

LEAGUE = COVENANT

A covenant consists of five elements:

- oath,

- written agreement,

- benefits,

- consequences,

- and signs.

This is modeled in scripture. Business today has utilized many of these truths as the basis for creating contracts. Tim experienced this in the Navy as war requires the highest level of covenant. Different levels of covenant require different levels of commitment. These are proportionate to the expected benefit or goal. The greater the purpose the higher the commitment.

THE GREATER THE PURPOSE THE HIGHER THE COMMITMENT.

In the early years of ministry, Tim and Brenda observed many abuses of covenant and membership. Because of that abuse, they eschewed membership for the first 20 years of their ministry. However, God began to reveal to them what was to come with regards to persecution, the war on the family, freedom of speech, and the need to connect the Church for the sake of increasing its ability to project power through prayer and strategic action.

The attack on religious freedom and marriage help provide context for the important restoration of the use of covenant in the Church today. As of today, the United State Supreme Court has just issued a verdict that redefines God's original design for marriage. How can the Church address the issue of the marriage covenant if it does not even understand or use it within the Church today? The following provides some context for the importance of the restoration of the use of covenant today.

Currently in the U.S., about 90% of churches and ministries have a 501(c)3 designation. Most do not know the history of our nation and how people like William Penn, the founder of Pennsylvania, was at one time imprisoned for preaching without a license. The founder of this state came here for the freedom to preach the gospel unhindered. For roughly 140+ years the Church in America existed as the "free Church." It was free, in that, civil government had no jurisdiction.

In fact, in 1811 the first church that sought civil government official recognition was the Episcopal Church. Back then, that took an act of Congress. Congress passed this on to President

James Madison who vetoed the bill saying essentially that civil government has no jurisdiction in Church government (Peter Kershaw, *In Caesar's Grip*, chapter 4, pp. 66).

WHO HAS CONTROL?

Here is a principle, what "you create," gives "you the right and the ability to legislate." In 1956 the 501(c)3 designation for charitable organizations was formed by our government and today most churches have chosen to use it. The U.S. government does nothing wrong when it defines the restrictions of the 501(c)3. It created it.

The wide spread use of this entity has given civil government more control within the Church at large. In a sense it is blurred the lines of jurisdiction between the Church and the civil government. It was reflected during recent deliberations regarding homosexual marriage in the Supreme Court when Justice Scalia said, "Is it conceivable that a minister who is authorized by the State to conduct marriage can decline to marry two men if indeed this Court holds that they have a constitutional right to marry?" (http://www.politico.com/ story/2015/04/supreme-court-gay-marriage-arguments-awkward-moments-117444.html#ixzz3bwcnJKkW)

Note the justice referred to a minister **authorized by "the State."** That is the view civil government is taking.

Tim says, "I am a minister of the Lord Jesus Christ and am charged with presenting His gospel of the kingdom. I am a citizen first in His kingdom and my authorization and power come from Him, not my civil government. I love this nation, I am thankful for this nation and I obey the laws." However, civil government is overstepping its bounds and the Church has invited this. Because of that Tim spent two years researching the law and IRS code. He discovered that according to the IRS, their ministry was actually functioning as a church and an association of churches and ministries. Since the law still made provision for a free church he developed a charter that reflected this reality; a covenant."

He did this because he believed it was an important step in positioning himself as a minister of Jesus Christ and to fully utilize the freedom found operating under the First Amendment to the United States Constitution. In the founding of this nation pastors and ministers regularly addressed moral issues in politics, but through civil governments' use of 501(c)3 status, they have been successful in muzzling the voice of a majority of the Church in this nation.

POSITIONED TO OBEY GOD

By not filing for a 501(c)3 designation, a critical step to proactively position KLI to address the attack on God's design for marriage was taken. Tim and the elders sought out a Constitutional attorney who understood Common Law and who also had understanding of Judaic Law. A man running for attorney general in Washington State was a perfect fit. Tim had him review our charter which forms the basis of our league. The attorney was quite impressed with what we had done, and the only changes he made was to suggest we actually copy certain portions of scripture into the charter rather than just reference the scripture as once read and the agreement by each member signed, we would be positioned to by-pass civil court on certain issues (such as marriage). We will have executed what our government calls an "alternative dispute resolution agreement."

One of the benefits for churches, networks, ministries, or organizations joining the "Kingdom League" will be the opportunity to use our charter to transition out of the non-profit corporation, 501(c) 3 status. Part of the goal is to position councils of elders in the gates of their local congregations and in their city to biblically perform the traditional role of a council of elders. Issues associated with marriage, reconciliation, and divorce certainly fall within that purview.

League = Covenant

Oath

Written Agreement

Benefits

Consequences

Signs

5

CHAPTER FIVE

International

International defines our geographic scope. We can serve leaders and churches in any city, region, or nation that shares a similar vision. KLI will empower Church leaders within cities, counties, parishes, regions, provinces, states, and even nations to establish their "league" within a geography associated with their kingdom assignment.

Our systems and strategies provide a way to facilitate local leaders cooperating together to transform their area through the presentation of the gospel of the kingdom of our Lord Jesus Christ, while simultaneously empowering them to stay connected to the larger body of Christ. In the last 20 years we've seen God use these strategies to mobilize and connect churches from Charismatic to Catholic, from Pentecostal to Presbyterian, and everything in between.

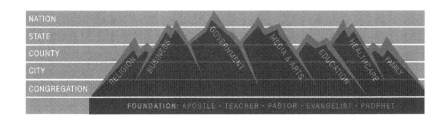

Kingdom League International is a federation of teams containing groups of people, churches, and ministries who are in covenant together to present the gospel of the kingdom anywhere on this planet. The manner in which we choose to express this is what makes us unique.

We believe that establishing God's government on earth as it is in heaven is best done by following the pattern King David set in the tabernacle on Mount Zion. Just as David organized and administrated teams of Levites to establish 24/7 prayer, praise and worship, KLI does the same. This taps into (or reproduces) the atmosphere of the heavenlies, and seats the courtroom of heaven. In addition, we also form councils in all spheres of society. A strategy we call **1Church1Day**.

We value those who dream and take risks, and encourage everyone to dream of solutions never modeled before. We urge each ministry or church to be bold and creative in their assigned call. While we value unique and different expressions, covenant with KLI requires participation in the overall strategy:

- to invite God's abiding presence,

- to establish the government of God in your city.

As the leader of a ministry this is accomplished by your organization (house church, church, ministry, or network) taking responsibility for:

- 24/7 prayer at least one day per month;

and/or

- you serving on one of the councils: church, business, government, media, education, healthcare, or family;

and/or

- encouraging people in your organization to serve on one of the strategic councils..

KLI MEMBERS ARE IN
COVENANT TOGETHER TO
PRESENT THE GOSPEL OF
THE KINGDOM ANYWHERE
ON THIS PLANET.

6

CHAPTER SIX

Our Missions

M issions describe the ways in which our vision will be
fulfilled. Many of the ministers, leaders, churches, and
ministries who connect with us major in one or more of the
missions below. They are the experts anointed in that field.
Our missions are to:

- City by city, empower independent saints with no
  local congregation, ministers and ministries, local
  congregations, and independent networks or denominations to interconnect in league with others who
  are passionate about demonstrating the gospel of the
  kingdom with character and supernatural power.

- Establish the government of the Lord through
  forming apostolic (strategic) councils representing

all 7 spheres of society and the fivefold ministry while establishing 24/7/365 prayer, praise, and worship.

- Plant and/or launch any ministry expression or auxiliary unit which supports the advancement of the gospel of the kingdom. Including, but not limited to, churches, apostolic resource centers, and city prayer centers.

- Establish training programs, schools, colleges, and educational courses that support local leaders in their efforts to make disciples who are kingdom transformers. We will prove, ordain, commission, charter, and send the equipped while we work to equip the called.

- Through a revelation of God's name as the Lord of Hosts, we will empower the Church to mobilize as the army of the Lord to project power to enforce the will of King Jesus.

- Publish the gospel of the kingdom of our Lord Jesus Christ through every media possible including but not limited to websites, e-newsletters, magazines, books, video, TV, and radio.

OUR VALUES & CULTURE

Our values help define our culture. It is how we choose to perform our vision and missions. These values include:

- **Love** – the preeminent value upon which all other values are based.

- **Jesus & His Kingdom** – we are passionate about representing Jesus and His kingdom.

- **The Church (Ekklesia)** – is the governmental assembly of called out ones, ambassadors united with a passion to represent the gospel of the kingdom in the character of Christ with signs and wonders confirming their word.

- **Honor** – we value and esteem all people.

- **Faith** – is love spoken and demonstrated through wisdom in action. Nothing is impossible.

- **Covenant Relationship** – is a relationship based on a holy agreement with God and a solemn commitment to people united by a common purpose. The league is an expression of that covenant relationship.

- **Presence of God** – is the preeminent focus of our pursuit.

- **Teamwork** – brings an exponential increase in gifts, anointing, and power.

- **Servant Leadership** – is the act of giving guidance and direction with the kingdom view.

- **Courage** – is the quality of mind and spirit which enables us to face difficulty, pain, or danger bravely without fear which affects our judgments or actions.

- **Commitment** – means we count the cost. Jesus gave His all and so should we.

- **Christ** – the anointing enables us to become joint heirs with Him.

- **Truth** – is a person (Jesus) and the truth is the Word of God. He is our ultimate standard, His Word is our ultimate model.

- **Stewardship** – is prioritized by people first, programs second, and buildings and stuff third.

- **Integrity** – refers to the adherence to moral and ethical principles, therefore we endeavor to develop Christ-like character.

- **Servants** – who serve faithfully are an essential expression of sonship.

- **Vision** – and personal destiny cannot be realized apart from an alignment with a corporate vision.

7

Methodology and Strategies

M ethodology refers to a set of systems of methods, principles, and rules for regulating a given discipline. Strategy refers to the science or art of combining and employing the means or war and in planning and directing large scale military movements.

Our methodologies and commitment to effective strategies are part of what make us unique in equipping leaders to mobilize and connect the body of Christ as an army in their respective cities and regions. God used Tim Taylor's career in the Navy as part of his training for ministry. God spoke to him in Operation Desert Storm about what was to come and after his return in 1991, he and Brenda visited Israel. While in Israel, two different prophets spoke of God's calling into the ministry.

God prepared Tim's destiny to carry a revelation of God's name as the Lord of Hosts (Armies). His very name Timothy Lewis Taylor speaks to this divine purpose. Timothy means "honor God," Lewis means "famous in war," and Taylor means "tailor." He is called to be a "team tailor" who equips the army of the Lord for victory and the glory and honor our Lord Jesus Christ. His wife's name, Brenda Sue Taylor, elaborates on their call. Brenda means "sword" and Sue means "graceful lily." This speaks to their call like holy eunuchs, to prepare the Church as a bride without spot, wrinkle, or blemish. The Church is called to be an army (Ezekiel 37:1-10, Joel 2:1-11, Ephesians 6:10-18) and the Church is called to be a bride (Matthew 25:1-10, Luke 5:34-35, John 3:29 and Revelation 18:23).

God prepared Tim to equip leaders with the ability to create strategy by teaching them the foundational principles of strategic war. In fact, Tim's naval career models the etymology of the Greek word translated apostle. It was first used as a Greek and Phoenician seafaring term for the leader of a convoy. Later, it came to mean the commander of an invasion force. Then it was used in reference to an ambassador general sent to represent a government (like Pontius Pilate was sent to Jerusalem to represent Rome). Lastly it was used by Jesus to identify certain disciples who were commissioned as "one sent."

Amazingly, Tim spent six years as a training officer in a convoy unit. He was deployed to Operation Desert Storm and served on the admiral's staff who oversaw all naval operations in the Persian Gulf, and he spent six weeks working out of an embassy.

This experience has given him a unique insight into scripture and its application in spiritual war.

> *"For though we walk in the flesh, we do not war according to the flesh. For the weapons of our warfare are not carnal but mighty in God for pulling down strongholds ..."*
>
> 2 CORINTHIANS 10:3-4

STRATEGY FOR WARFARE

The word translated "war" comes from the Greek word *strateuomai* which according to *Strong's Concordance* means "to serve in a military campaign ... to execute the apostulate ..." *Apostulate* literally means the office of apostle. The word translated "warfare" comes from the Greek word *strateia* which according to *Strong's* means "military service, the apostolic career ..." This Greek word serves as the root of our word for "strategy" today.

God made the apostle gift for strategy and strategy is required in war. This gift includes a gift of revelation along with a gift of wisdom. Wisdom is an essential component of building and war (Proverbs 24:3-6).

An army is not made up of individual warriors, but rather soldiers who are organized into teams or units. This becomes an essential element of increasing our ability to project power to enforce the will of King Jesus. God equipped Tim through the Navy War College as He showed Him the biblical basis for every principle of war they taught. These principles undergird every methodology and serve as the basis for every strategy. It has been proven through leaders, churches, and ministries in over 36 nations with supernatural, reproducible, measurable results following them.

The methodologies we use are not new, but rather a new expression of an ancient pattern. What follows are some of the things God spoke to Tim during an encounter in 2008 followed by some brief descriptions.

8

CHAPTER EIGHT

Apostolic Resource Centers — ARCs

In December 2007 Tim was sharing a cup of coffee with Jason Hubbard who in May 2008 became the first of more than 31 city prayer centers launched through the Operation Rolling Thunder strategy. Jason asked Tim what he saw God doing in 2008. An anointing fell upon Tim as he answered and prophesied with Luke 17:26-30 in mind which says:

> *"So as it was in the days of Noah, so shall it be before the coming of the Son of Man. They ate, they drank, they married wives, they were given in marriage, until the day that Noah entered the ark, and the flood came and destroyed them all. Even so will it be in the day when the Son of Man is revealed."*

Then Tim heard the Lord say, "Noah built Me an ark, and I want you to be an ARC – an Apostolic Resource Center. Only God does not just want an ARC, He wants a fleet of ARCs." Tim knew his assignment was to develop a pattern that facilitates the establishment of many ARCs.

Using his background in the Navy to communicate, the Lord showed Tim that the ARC was not one vessel, but is best illustrated using an air craft carrier task force. It is a team of teams or a team of units functioning together as one. This task force is mobile. Each ship has a specialized function it performs. Each ship has the same command structure and roles filled. The aircraft carrier hosts a strategic operations center and maintains a 24/7 combat air patrol. While it has its own captain and crew, the aircraft carrier often serves as the command ship for an admiral and staff that are responsible for the mission of that task force. The task force is connected through a strategic communication system which facilitates disciplined orderly teamwork within that task force to project power to enforce the will of the government it represents.

THE ARC IS A TEAM OF UNITS FUNCTIONING TOGETHER AS ONE.

The ARC that Tim sees is the church and the church is the ARC. The difference compared to traditional congregations has to do with the way the different ministries and congregations function together as one. Many different parts, yet one body for one purpose for the glory of King Jesus'.

The ARC reflects the apostolic nature of God. It is a mobilization strategy for the army of the Lord. During that time the Lord showed Tim how He wanted to gather the elders at the gates of a city. The elders would start with 12 general councils representing the 7 spheres of society and the fivefold ministry. The presence of God would be preeminent. It's like the heavenly city that comes down in Revelation 21:10-12.

"And he carried me away in the Spirit to a great and high mountain, and showed me the great city, the holy Jerusalem, descending out of heaven from God, having the glory of God. Her light was like a most precious stone, like a jasper stone, clear as crystal. Also she had a great and high wall with twelve gates, and twelve angels at the gates ..."

Who sits in the gate? The Bible teaches us that kings and elders sit in the gate. These are the leaders who decide what comes in and out of a city or a ministry.

All of KLI's systems and strategies are designed to assist leaders within their respective leagues (i.e. city, county, state ...) to establish their ARC; their Apostolic (strategic) Resource Center. It facilitates kingdom teamwork in their local area while staying connected to and even working with the larger body of Christ.

GOD GIVES A SIGN

After Tim's encounter with the Lord that day Brenda came home from work. As they walked out to their office to see what the Lord showed Tim they watched a sign and a wonder. Just before they entered the office two hummingbirds appeared. The female sat on the arbor while the male hummingbird flew around in big circles. Tim joked, "Look, he is flying in an arc."

Brenda shared with Tim the following day how that her research showed that they had witnessed the mating ritual of the hummingbirds. The male would fly in a circle making a big "arc" to show the female how strong he was.

The Lord showed them that the hummingbird was a sign. Just like the male made a big arc because he was trying to attract a bride, so God was calling people to make ARCs because He is preparing a bride for His son. Revelation 21:2-4 says:

Then I, John, saw the holy city, New Jerusalem, coming down out of heaven from God, prepared as a bride adorned for her husband. And I heard a loud voice from heaven saying, "Behold, the tabernacle of God is with men, and He will dwell with them, and they shall be His people. God Himself will be with them and be their God. And God will wipe away every tear from their eyes; there shall be no more death, nor sorrow, nor crying. There shall be no more pain, for the former things have passed away."

Here are the characteristics of the ARC that Tim saw. It included or serves:

- 31 churches/house churches/ministries who will build a wall of prayer family by family with each church or ministry covering one day each month with 24/7 prayer.

- 12 apostolic councils representing church, business, government, media/arts/entertainment, education, healthcare, the family as well as apostle, prophet, evangelist, pastor and teacher.

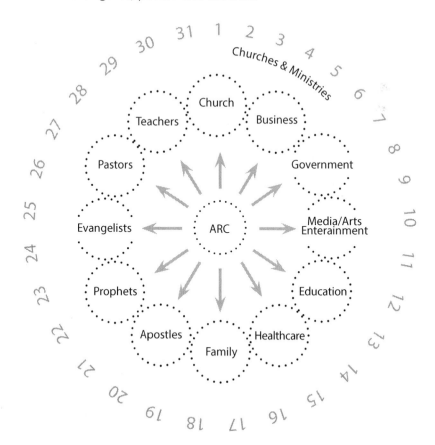

- Ministers trained to pastor, make disciples and oversee each house church, ministry or home meeting.

- A communications hub interconnecting house churches, home meetings, ministries and saints in a city/ county or regional Church. The hub also interconnects with other ARCs.

- A training center encouraging, supporting, and equipping church planters, strategic leaders, and intercessors representing every sphere of society and the fivefold ministry utilizing as much as possible the local gifts God deposited in people He placed in that community.

- A strategic operations center communicating, coordinating, and facilitating the gathering of spiritual intelligence and supporting the strategic councils formed to represent the 7 spheres of society and the fivefold ministry. As strategic prayer and action plans are developed the ARC facilitates the mobilization of the people and the implementation and coordination of the plan under the direction of their councils.

- A resource center where the gifts, talents, abilities, and anointings in people are assessed and prepared for distribution into their community.

- A resource center where financial and practical resources are received and distributed.

- City or regional houses of prayer that reflect the type of continual prayer, praise and worship represented in David's tabernacle.

- Healing rooms, crisis pregnancy centers and any other ministry that might be referred to as "para-church" with the Church in the city/region.

- The capacity to create or support the Church's role in presenting the gospel of the kingdom of our Lord Jesus Christ in character and power through His people in each of the 7 spheres. This includes unique business concepts, entities, or any type of creative media or solution founded on God's wisdom and His love.

MEETING CHARACTERISTICS

Each church/meeting functions like a Special Forces team whose number one mission is training. They provide the primary place for:

- Community

- Family

- Discipleship, teaching, training, mentoring

- Service

- Proving leaders (1 Thess. 5:21, 2 Tim. 2:2, Luke 19:17-18, Matt. 20:26-28)

- Weekly worship

- Takes one day per month to build the wall of prayer with the ARC in their city/region.

The previous descriptions are some of the main points. The list is not comprehensive.

- Methodology

  » Covenant or Leagues level of covenant

  » The 1Church1Day Community Prayer Transformation System: www.1Church1Day.org

  » First & Second Kingdom Congress—mp3s

9

CHAPTER NINE

The Key of David

———————————————————————————

G od has called and equipped Tim as a strategist with an
apostolic assignment. That assignment is to restore
David's fallen tabernacle. The tabernacle of David is the key
of David: God's abiding presence. It was the first decision King
David made when he began to expand the kingdom of Israel. It
is a type and shadow. For a complete explanation listen to "The
Apostles' Revelation of David's Tabernacle" (available at www.
kingdomleague.org). This message describes Peter's revelation
on the day of Pentecost (Acts 2) and the role it played in the
birth of the Church.

Following is a diagram that represents the simplicity of this
strategy:

The restoration of David's tabernacle is the key to the harvest. Here's how:

- It is the organization and administration of people to create the atmosphere of heaven on earth so that God's abiding presence will be welcome.

- It seats the courtroom of heaven so that cases can be pleaded through intercession.

- It positions the Church to hear God's decision and then give voice to it on earth as it is in heaven.

David's tabernacle was established on Mount Zion in the City of David. 2 Samuel 5:7 calls it a stronghold and *Strong's*

Concordance says that the Hebraic term for city literally means a place guarded by a watch. It is important to note that in every reformation recorded in scripture they all reverted to David's pattern. Nehemiah was one of those restorers and God showed Tim a modern way to apply an ancient pattern which empowers congregations/ministries to work together to build a wall of prayer and establish a watch in their city. For more information see the book, *Build the Wall* in KLI's online store.

EVERY REFORMATION RECORDED IN SCRIPTURE REVERTED BACK TO DAVID'S PATTERN.

Mount Zion is the holy mountain where God's house of prayer for all nations is located (Isaiah 56:7, Psalm 2:6 & Joel 3:17). It is the mountain which shall be established on top of all the other mountains (Isaiah 2:2-3). God showed Tim a methodology whereby churches in any city or region can occupy the mountain of the Lord's house of prayer for all nations 24/7/365 quickly and efficiently. KLI is applying this pattern within this network as well.

- Methodology

  » "Build the Wall" of prayer

  » Developing Apostolic Strategy

  » Strategic Leadership – 8 Apostolic Principles of War

GOD'S ABIDING
PRESENCE IS
THE KEY.

10

CHAPTER TEN

Gathering Elders at the Gates of all 7 Spheres of Society

In the early 2000s God began to speak to Tim about the 7 spheres of society. Later he discovered that Dr. Loren Cunningham (YWAM) and Dr. Bill Bright (Campus Crusade for Christ) had shared about their vision regarding the 7 mountains 25 years earlier. Dr. Lance Wallnau carries that message regarding the 7 mountains today.

The 7 spheres the Lord showed Tim consisted of church, business, government, media/arts/entertainment, education, healthcare and the family. While these spheres are slightly different from the 7 mountains, the concept is basically the same. Remembering that the old is a type and shadow and that these things were written for our learning, Tim looks for patterns in God's word which enable Christians today to put the revelation and their faith into action.

King David was Solomon's father and Solomon was the author of Proverbs. Solomon writes, "By wise council build and by wise council wage war" (Proverbs 24:3-6). Gathering elders in councils was used in civil as well as religious government in Hebraic culture. Proverbs also says there is safety in the multitude of council and God designed us to need each other (Ephesians 4:16, Ezekiel 37:1-10 and 1 Corinthians 12).

Beginning in 2005, Tim began to use Operation Rolling Thunder (1Church1Day) as a way to gather the elders at the gates by forming councils representing all 7 spheres within each jurisdiction (church, city, county, state ...). This methodology initiates a process that over time helps discover the strategic gifts (apostolic and prophetic) God pre-deployed and assigned to that community. They are essential to discovering God's divine plan for each respective community.

Elders are gathered at the gates make decisions (Deuteronomy 21:19, 22:15, Joshua 20:4). They are smarter together than apart so they are formed into councils. The church council also includes five ministry gifts which form councils as well; apostle, prophet, teacher, pastor and evangelist which when combined with the other spheres gives us a goal of 12.

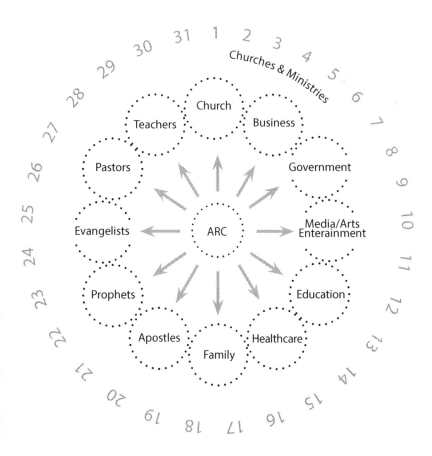

The 24/7 prayer invites God who is also the Spirit of Wisdom, Understanding, Council and Might (Isaiah 11: 2) into the presence of these councils. "The Lord founded Zion" (Isaiah 14:32). The word "founded" in the Hebrew means to found, sit down together, and consult. God created Zion so that He could sit down and consult with the elders and leaders within a community.

This is an important element in establishing God's kingdom on earth.

Isaiah 9:6 prophesies about Jesus telling us that the government will rest upon His shoulders. Jesus gave the Church a government and five unique gifts to equip the saints for the work of the ministry. Part of the Church government's assignment is to provide and atmosphere that welcomes God's abiding presence into a community. That is what King David did in the City of David on Mount Zion. This creates a place for God's throne to be set. This is why James the apostle said in Acts 15:16 that in the latter days God would restore David's tabernacle. It is a key to God's government being established on earth.

The Ark of the Covenant is a type of God's presence. It was at the center of the Tabernacle of David. The ark was only to be carried on the shoulders of the Levites. The Levites are a type and shadow of the five-fold ministry today. It is the responsibility of the Church government to provide a foundation for God's house to be built.

The Bible says there is wisdom in a multitude of council and by wise council we are to build and to wage war (Proverbs 24:3-6). Proverbs 8:1-2 tells us that wisdom takes it's stand on top of a high hill (think MT Zion) and cries out at the gates of a city. Proverbs 9:1 says that wisdom has built her house and hewn her 7 pillars.

Building a House of Prayer

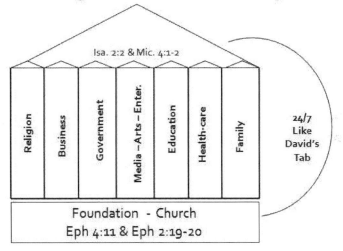

What is this house that we are building? It is the mountain of the Lord's house of prayer for all nations. The foundation is laid by the apostles and prophets with Jesus Christ being the Chief Cornerstone (Ephesians 2:19-21). The pillars of this house are formed through these councils. The roof or covering is the canopy of 24/7 prayer raised up 365 days a year. It is difficult for any one ministry to do this alone but if the local churches and ministries work together it is possible to sustain this.

Councils work best with anywhere from two to twelve people. Any more and it becomes unwieldy. Therefore part of the structure and plan includes a way for the councils to be multiplied. The 12 councils presented here are not the end, but rather the beginning.

If real disciples and leaders fill these roles on these councils then they will make disciples who make disciples. As the councils grow they can become more specific. For example, business could multiply into aerospace, biotech, software, automotive, retail, wholesale, etc. The only limit is the creative imagination of God's people and asking God what would He like to see in each specific area. There is no end to the number of councils that are formed. It depends upon the vision of the local leadership to steward that.

This is one way to see this manifest:

> *"Of the increase of His government and peace there will be no end, Upon the throne of David and over His kingdom, To order it and establish it with judgment and justice from that time forward, even forever. The zeal of the Lord of hosts will perform this."*
>
> ISAIAH 9:7 NKJV

- Methodology

  » 1Church1Day

  » Developing Apostolic Strategy

  » Strategic Leadership – 8 Apostolic Principles of War

IT IS THE RESPONSIBILITY
OF THE CHURCH
GOVERNMENT TO PROVIDE
A FOUNDATION FOR GOD'S
HOUSE TO BE BUILT.

11

The Church is an Army

Jesus really shook up the religious world by using words from other cultures, like the word *apostolos* or apostle. As we learned previously this term was used first as the leader of a convoy, then the commander of an invasion force, and later it referred to an ambassador general. Apostle was a military term in Jesus' day. In Matthew 16:18 Jesus introduces ecclesia or Church.

Ecclesia was the principle assembly of the democracy of ancient Athens around 480 BC. It was open to all men who had at least two years of military service. They were responsible for making governmental decisions, declaring war, and developing military strategy. While a building was built to host their meetings, the *ecclesia* was not the building but rather the gathering of people united in a common purpose.

The Church of Jesus Christ is not a physical building but rather a people who are called out to govern and represent His gospel of the kingdom. The Church was made for spiritual war and the issue at hand are the souls of men and women and their eternal destiny in heaven or in hell.

> .... *For this purpose the Son of God was manifested, that He might destroy the works of the devil.*
>
> 1 JOHN 3:8

This is why the Church needs apostolic gifts today. God designed the apostle along with the office of prophet for spiritual war.

In scripture we see Church referring to a gathering of the ecclesia in a home, in a city, or in a region. Finally, there is the Church which is made up of all congregations from around the world as well as those believers who have preceded us into glory.

At KLI we foresaw the coming persecution and believe that the house Church is an integral part of God's strategy for these days. There will always be larger congregations, but we strongly urge them to implement a small group strategy similar to the manner in which we seek to connect many local house churches and ministries. It is one of the best ways to engage everyone in ministry.

KLI provides 1Church1Day as a strategic communication plan that networks these small congregations into a mighty, powerful army. It enables these small units to connect and collaborate together to impact their city and beyond.

Connecting individual believers to God
through an intimate, personal prayer life

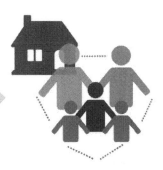

Uniting families through
prayer in the home

Strengthening the local church
with family-to-family prayer.

Connecting the Church in the
city and bringing God's abiding
presence through 24/7 prayer.

The Lord gave the word; great was the company of those who proclaimed it.

PSALM 68:11

- Methodology

    » **1Church1Day** Community Prayer Transformation System

    » **Developing Apostolic Strategy**

    » **Build the Wall**

    » **Operation Rolling Thunder – revised edition**

    » **The Apostolic Reformation**

    » **The Kingdom Academy**

12

CHAPTER TWELVE

Church Government

Jesus gave us a government for the Church and gifts to equip the Church for service. The gifts come our heavenly Father (Romans 12:1-8), Jesus (Ephesians 4:11), and the Holy Spirit (1 Corinthians 12:1-11). The fivefold gifts of apostle, prophet, evangelist, pastor and teacher were given to equip the saints for the work of the ministry (*diakonia*). Everyone is called to serve or minister in some capacity.

God gave the Church government to give good stewardship and oversight to God's purpose, the corporate employment of each group, and equipping so that each person has the opportunity to fulfill their destiny. Each person has a role and Ephesians 4:16 teaches us that when every part does their share it edifies the body in love.

The apostle and prophet were teamed together. Whenever God wants to pioneer a new concept, develop a new strategy, mobilize the Church for spiritual war, and establish a congregation where one did not exist the apostolic and prophetic gifts are needed. God uses them to lay the foundation (Ephesians 2:19-22) for effective teamwork among the other gifts.

1 Corinthians 12:28 speaks to an order of function more so than to a hierarchy.

God set firstly apostles, secondarily prophets, thirdly teachers, after that miracles, then gifts of healing ...

Paul the apostle gives us a great example where he had helped pioneer a couple of works. In 1 Timothy, Paul gives Timothy a charge for Ephesus and in Titus. He charges him to set Crete in order. In 1 Timothy 3 and Titus 1 we find the following terms; *episkopos* (bishop or overseer), *presbuteros* (elder) and *diakanos* (minister or deacon).

The kingdom in which we exist is a theocracy. A king rules. A king appoints. In this case King Jesus is our king. We seek to ascertain His will and recognize what He is doing by and through

Holy Spirit. Hence we see Paul appointing Timothy and Titus to their respective assignments. No doubt this selection was done through council and applying 1 Thessalonians 5:21 and 2 Timothy 2:2 wherein Paul admonishes us to entrust the ministry to proven people.

Timothy and Titus were each responsible to carry out the assigned vision though each vision would require many people performing their role. While their assignment was the same their assigned territory was different.

Church government (ie. congregation/ministry) consists of a council of elders with one, an equal among their peers, serving as the overseer—the primary steward, the bishop of the vision for that specific work or portion of the church. Character is critical as a theocratic form of government, while very efficient, is one of the forms most easily abused. The solution to guard against abuse is servant leadership with safeguards.

These truths are reflected in our charter and are modeled in KLI. Any church or ministry who is called to covenant with KLI will have the ability to adopt this charter as well. Tim foresaw that many ministers would desire to opt out of their status as a non-profit corporation in order to clarify the confused jurisdictional lines between the Church and civil government now and in the coming days

KLI's church government is as follows: We have a council of elders who hold a variety of fivefold ministry gifts. Each gift mix brings a unique perspective of God's heart to issues that arise.

When combined together there is a greater chance of receiving the whole of God's counsel on an issue.

ROLE OF THE BISHOP

There is a "set one" (Numbers 27:16) who serves as the bishop or overseer of the vision and the council. The bishop is selected by the Lord and is ultimately held accountable for KLI's success or failure. It is like a ship's Captain in the U.S. Navy. It doesn't matter who is doing what nor where the captain is, if the Third Mate drives the ship aground, the Captain is the one held ultimately responsible. He can be court-martialed and lose his command. This is why at sea, the Captain has the final word. We find a similar pattern modeled in the Old Testament (ie. Moses, Joshua, King David ...) as well as in Acts 15 by James the apostle.

Therefore, because the bishop is ultimately responsible before the Lord for the vision's success or failure, the bishop has the final say in each decision. Good leadership requires that the bishop use wisdom in drawing the gold out of each elder before decisions are made.

THE ACCOUNTABILITY COUNCIL

To protect the Church and ministry from the moral failure or abuse of the bishop's power, an accountability council was established outside of KLI. This council is made up of respected proven elders/ministers outside of KLI who have a personal relationship with the bishop. This council has the authority to prescribe counsel, correction and, if necessary, removal from ministry.

MORE TO THE STORY ...

The vision of KLI's government is still in process as of this printing. When the goal is reached there will be 12 councils each representing one of the fivefold gifts (apostle, prophet, evangelist, pastor and teacher) and the 7 spheres (church/religion, business, government, media/entertainment/arts, education, healthcare and family. Ideally, the chair of each of these councils will have an apostolic gift and will form the council of elders previously referenced for KLI.

Apostles and prophets work together to found ... new works!

The bishop/overseer (*episkopos*) and the elders (*presbuteros*) are the decision makers. They form the government. In the beginning of a new work, an apostle working with prophets plays a much greater role in the direction and founding. Once an overseer and council of elders are set in place, the role of the apostle changes. This is much like the role changes between a father and son when the son matures and has his own family. The dynamic of the relationship changes as the son oversees and leads his family. The father, though highly honored and respected, for the sake of giving glory to God, takes on more of an advisory role.

Role of the Deacon

In American Church culture it seems as if the role of deacon was confused with the function of elders in some denominations and in others, regulated to the role of performing practical duties such as cleaning a building, mowing the lawn, handling finances ... It's true, we need men and women performing these services and they should carry the character qualifications similar to elders. However, a *diakanos* is a minister in the sense of ministering the word of God also. For example, Paul and Apollos were called ministers in 1 Corinthians 3:5 and in Romans 16:1 Phebe is a *diakanos* to the church at Cenchrea.

Everyone ought to aspire to have the character of an elder and everyone is called to be a minister (Ephesians 4;12). The *diakanos* can carry any variety of gifts (Romans 12, Ephesians 4, and 1 Corinthians 12) and minister practically and also in teaching as modeled by Paul, Apollos, Tychicus, Timothy ... however, they are not responsible for making governmental decisions.

13

The Church Verses the Non-Profit

S ome of the information to be presented is specific to the Church in America. However, the principles presented are universal and eternal.

First, there is nothing wrong with a non-profit corporation. Tim and Brenda oversaw Watchman Ministries International which was a 501(c)3 for 20 years. However, Tim was challenged by the government a non-profit was required to operate. Tim was the president, Brenda the vice-president, and a variety of others filled different roles on the board. He could not find those *terms president, vice president, secretary,* or *board member* in the Bible. This led him on a journey into the history of the Church in America, the history of 501(c)3, and an extensive look at the IRS code.

The Church in America came here for religious freedom. They were seeking to escape the oppressive government of England wherein the king also served as the head of the church. Laws were introduced which required all ministers to be licensed. A license was required to preach to more than five people. For example, did you know that William Penn, a Quaker, the founder of Pennsylvania was at one time imprisoned in England because he violated that law? He came to America for religious liberty.

For over 140 years congregations in America were called "free churches." They were free from civil government. But in 1811 the Episcopal Church sought to be approved by—endorsed by—civil government. Then it took an act of Congress. James Madison was president at that time, and his response gives us keen insight into the issue. When the bill reached his desk he vetoed it basically saying that civil government has no jurisdiction in Church government. He understood this principle:

What you create, you have the right and ability to legislate.

The federal government did not create the Church. Jesus did! Jesus gave the Church a government. Madison understood the principle of jurisdiction.

A February 11, 1990 *New York Times* article by Martin Tolchin called "How Johnson Won The Election He'd Lost" says that Johnson won the election by fraud. It helps us envision Johnson's motive for introducing a bill that created the 501(c)3. There were a couple of non-profits who sought to expose his fraud, so Johnson introduced the bill to help limit their speech as it pertains to politics. Apparently, though churches were not the target, they were added to the list and the bill was passed with no deliberation on the floor of the house in 1954.

As of today roughly 90% of churches are 501(c)3 non-profit corporations. Why did so many churches do this? At first, some churches did it because only 501(c)3s were eligible to apply for federal grants. They wanted access to the money. Civil government encouraged it because it meant licensing and licensing is a source of revenue and gives them more control. As time went on it created more business for attorneys and accountants who pay taxes. Then it was introduced to the education system and by the time you reach the 1980s, most had forgotten how the Church in America started. The terms "church" and "501c3" became synonymous. The concept of "free church" was virtually forgotten.

Think about the principle of creation presented in Genesis 1:11-13. The grass, herbs, and trees all produce seeds which yield fruit "according to its kind." The seed reproduces the characteristics of the host. In verse 24 and 25 the animals follow the same pattern.

The 501(c)3 is the seed from the Federal Government and it produces after its own kind: president, vice-president, secretary etc. Jesus produced the Church and the Church should produce after its own kind—don't you agree?

In John 12:23-28, Jesus likens himself to a seed that must die. Once that seed was planted it sprouted up in three days. Fifty days later (Acts 2) it was harvested when three thousand souls were added to His Church. The Church is to reflect the attributes of Jesus. Colossians 2:9 says that Jesus fully embodied the Godhead. He is our Apostle and the High Priest of our profession. He is the great Pastor (Shepherd), Rabbi (Teacher), Prophet and Evangelist. He is the Bishop/Overseer/Episkopos of our soul.

The fruitfulness of Watchman Ministries International (WMI) also played a factor in Tim's research of the IRS code. Many houses of prayer and church plants from those houses of prayer were reported for years, and some began to call themselves the WMI family of churches and ministries. When Tim compared that to the 13 characteristics that the IRS code looks at when attempting to identify a church he found that WMI was, by their definition, a church and an association of churches and ministries. They agreed!

Once an understanding of Church history in America was acquired, they realized they had invited civil government into the mix with Church government. The lines of jurisdiction were muddled between the Church and civil government and they believed that in order to position themselves to fully re-present the gospel of the kingdom of Jesus Christ, they needed to correct this.

An apostolic council was held in February 2011 with elders, apostles, and prophets in attendance wherein they sought the

Lord to determine how they should respond. It was determined that it was time to transition from Watchman Ministries International into Kingdom League International. Tim, with the assistance of elders, wrote a charter. He also foresaw the attack on marriage and religious freedom and in 2011 sought out an attorney who understood common law, Constitutional law, and Judaic law.

After a review of the Kingdom League International Charter it was approved and KLI was established as a church and an association of churches and ministries. *(IRS Code 508(c)(1)(a) addresses the issue of churches.)*

The government of KLI reflects the government Christ established. Hence, Tim is not the president but rather the founding apostle. He also fills the role as its bishop or overseer and is preparing KLI to be handed over to the next generation while continuing to reproduce what Christ has begun in them.

THE FEDERAL
GOVERNMENT
DID NOT CREATE
THE CHURCH,
JESUS DID!

14

Covenant Relationships = League

In doing research for KLI's charter, Tim was inspired by *The Triumph of Justice*. He was focused on two areas; the role of elders, and the expected attack on God's institution of marriage. Published by Morningstar Publications in 2008, this book was written by an Orthodox Jewish Rabbi who'd come to know Jesus. In the chapter, "Practical Steps: Taking Marriage Back," the author compared the divorce rate in Christendom with Jews who actually practiced Judaism in America. He stated that Barna reported the divorce rate in Christendom close to 50% while within the Jewish community it was only 3%. Why was there a disparity when in Judaism divorce is allowed?

There were a few factors, but the one that caught Tim's immediate attention was the role of elders (or a council of elders) connected to a covenant agreement. This subject is much too extensive to delve into here, however, the conclusion was that the biblical role of elders as defined in scripture was performed. Marriage was one of the areas they were responsible to address, and a covenant agreement was essential for their system to work.

The covenant agreement created a membership whereby (in the eyes of the civil government) they could choose to address a variety of issues through their own agreement and this includes marriage. A covenant creates what civil government calls "an alternative dispute resolution process" for the members. This allows the troubled people and the council of elders to bypass civil court on certain issues (ie. civil not criminal) such as marriage within the faith community.

Restoring the biblical role of a council of elders is fundamental for the Church to lay a foundation for gathering the elders in the gates. The Church lays the foundation and is responsible to set and hold the moral standard. In KLI the Church council is composed of five other councils: apostle, prophet, evangelist, pastor, and teacher. It is upon this foundation that the councils for business, government, media, education, healthcare, and the family are formed.

The word translated covenant can also be translated league. This covenant agreement combined with a common communication protocol is the connective tissue that holds KLI together. It is like the ligaments described in Ezekiel 37. It attaches the bones together. It is critical for the internal foundation that supports life. It is the first step in seeing the body connected so that it raises up an exceeding great and mighty army (Ezekiel 37:10). It lays the covenantal foundation for the Church(es) who have leagued together to address covenantal disputes in marriage, business, or other areas of life. The Apostle Paul says in 1 Corinthians 6:1-2 (NKJV):

> *"Dare any of you, having a matter against another, go to law before the unrighteous, and not before the saints? Do you not know that the saints will judge the world? And if the world will be judged by you, are you unworthy to judge the smallest matters?"*

COVENANT RELATIONSHIP WITHIN KLI

There are five biblical elements to covenant. There is a written portion, the oath, benefits, consequences, and signs of covenant. The charter is the written covenant. It is how a person or a ministry enters into this Kingdom League. The charter identifies those five elements.

We see our role as stewarding a sacred trust. We recognize that we represent a portion of Christ's church. The point is this: it is not our church, but rather His. We are to function in a sense like holy eunuchs preparing a bride to meet her bridegroom. We will not touch Christ's bride in an unholy fashion.

At the same time we are charged with connecting His Church as one and mobilizing that bride as a mighty army. The standard is high and the cause is just. The issue at hand are the souls of men and women and their eternal destiny in heaven or in hell. We are mobilizing a kingdom army who'll carry and demonstrate the gospel of the kingdom of our Lord Jesus Christ. We seek to save, disciple, and then redeploy those disciples as ministers back into the harvest.

Because of this, the process of entering into covenant is not easy. Like the US Marine Corps we seek the few that desire to live up to the standard their motto reflects: "*semper fidelis*" or always faithful. The process is not easy but it is worth it. There are three types of covenant relationship within KLI. The first three deal with those who are called to part of the core KLI team. The last type is for those who start or become part of a city, county, parish, regional, province, state, or national league.

FELLOW WORKERS

Fellow Workers make up the largest part of the team and also represents the lowest level of covenant. Individuals, families and ministries who share our vision are invited to join the League as a Fellow Worker. This integral part of the KLI team helps provide the necessary foundation for our ministry efforts through regular offerings and prayer. KLI is a pioneer and is oftened likened unto the point of the spear. The size of this team plays a critical role in determining the amount of mass or power behind the point. Those who become part of this team, receive prioritized prayer support, first access to KLI news and resources, and an invitation to join us on our own 1Church1Day prayer watch.

TRIBE MEMBER

Tribe Members can be fivefold and seven-sphere church leaders who view one or more of KLI's leaders as a mentor, teacher, or advisor, but your ordination or commissioning has come from another church or ministry. Though not ordained or commissioned through KLI, Tribe Members seek additional expertise and covering and desire KLI to be part of their core advisory team and available to them during challenges as they arise. Tribe Members receive prayer support, strategic counseling, the opportunity to function as part of a kingdom team and our pledge to stand with you in battle. You are invited to join the KLI Tribe. This level of covenant requires signing the KLI Charter.

FAMILY MEMBER

For those desiring a closer level of relationship with KLI, we invite you to join us as a Family Member. This level of involvement includes members of our local base-of-operations church, ministers ordained or commissioned through KLI, or leaders overseeing operations in their city, state, or nation. Family Members receive 24/7 prayer support, strategic counseling, access to our apostolic resources, and our pledge to stand with you in battle. This level of covenant requires signing the KLI Charter.

WHAT IS INVOLVED TO JOIN KLI?

If you would like to league with KLI or learn more visit **http://www.kingdomleague.org/join-the-league.html**. Your primary oath and allegiance is to the Lord. What follows below is an example of the oath that Tribe or Family members take when they join KLI.

I declare that:

1. I have accepted Jesus as your Lord and Savior

2. I have been Water Baptized (by full emersion)

3. I agree to abide by the conditions set forth in the charter

4. I agree to the Statement of Faith

5. I request to relate to KLI as a _____ Member
   (please write in Family or Tribe)

6. I commit to pray for KLI and give regularly _____
   (please indicate the amount or percent of your planned contribution/support to KLI)

"I _____ (*print your name*), do solemnly declare that I have accepted Jesus Crhist as both my Lord and Savior, I have been water baptized, I have read and agree to abide by the Kingdom League International Charter. I commit that I will support and advance the gosepl of the kingdom of our Lord Jesus Christ as I take my place within this league. I commit to using my gifts, talents, abilities, and resources to build the kingdom of God.

I will become all I can be in the army of the Lord and will strive to fulfill my personal destiny in Christ while helping others find their destiny as part of a team. I willfully take my position in His army, the family of God, and this team. I will be all for one, King Jesus, and we will be one for all, the Church, the Ekklesia, the called-out ones.

I commit to becoming a disciple of Christ, a servant leader, and exercising my faith to see His character formed within me while His power flows through me. I commit to making disciples after Jesus Christ and upholding the Bible as the infallible word of God. I will bear true faith and allegiance to the Lord Jesus Christ, His Church, and this league to which I am entering into covenant. I take this obligation freely, without any mental reservation or purpose of of evasion, so help me God."

Signed: _____ Date: _____

Witness 1: _____ Date: _____

Witness 2: _____ Date: _____

The strength of KLI comes from unity of purpose (John 17:21) and focused strategy behind a cause. KLI meaningfully connects and mobilizes those who are passionate about God's abiding presence and committed to re-present the gospel of the kingdom of our Lord Jesus Christ.

THE KINGDOM LEAGUE

Over the last decade, we have pioneered a mobilization strategy called 1Church1Day (formerly called Operation Rolling Thunder). This strategy has been used by leaders in over 36 nations to mobilize and connect the Church in a city, county, province, region, or state to establish 24/7 prayer while forming strategic councils. In every community where there is long term transformation occurring, we found there was a certain level of covenant. Not many cities enjoy long term growing examples of transformation.

This league refers to a "Kingdom League." This is distinctly different from the Family, Tribe, or Fellow Workers which describe people who desire to connect directly with KLI. The goal here is to provide a minimum level of covenant while supporting the connecting of the many diverse parts of the Church passionate about transforming their city or region through the presentation of the gospel of the kingdom of our Lord Jesus Christ. This is done by empowering leaders to form a league for a city, county, province, region, or state.

Please think of the league in the same way you would think of the National Football League, National Soccer League, or Major League Baseball. Each team has total ownership of their organization and determines how it will train and operate. Each team has the same positions, their own plays, and their distinctive culture. Each member of each team is responsible for their own performance, and each team is only as good as its players, coaches, and support staff. At the same time they've joined a league—agreeing to abide by certain rules and uphold certain standards of play. In our case we desire to see all teams operate within a kingdom culture that honors Jesus Christ as He is the King of Kings, and we desire to re-present Him.

This Kingdom League empowers leaders who desire to use the 1Church1Day strategy to mobilize the Church in their area of responsibility as a way to form a league for their geographic location. We have seen this strategy facilitate uniting the Church in cities around the world from Charismatic to Catholic, and from Presbyterian to Pentecostal. This strategy—combined with covenant—will facilitate the networking of networks, connecting diverse streams and denominations who are passionate about seeing a league of churches and ministries united to transform their community long term through strategic prayer and action.

This Kingdom League provides a pattern that facilitates the formation of church or ministry teams and councils. A league can be established in city, county, province, state, or region. Following is an overview of the teams.

Church teams include:

- Churches, house churches, and ministries.
- Houses of Prayer
- Healing Rooms
- Bible Schools, Seminaries, and Institutes

Councils Include:

- Government
- Business
- Media, Arts, Entertainment
- Education
- Healthcare
- Family
- Church
  - Apostle
  - Prophet
  - Pastor
  - Teacher

12 COUNCILS

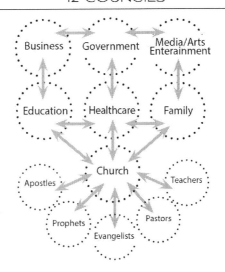

This league serves to promote and foster the primary business of King Jesus which includes inviting God's abiding presence into a city through 24/7 prayer, praise, and worship while also gathering the elders at the gates. Our 1Church1Day model has proven effective in helping communities establish continual prayer while the councils serve as our way of gathering the elders at the gates of a modern city. These councils of strategic leaders play an important role in developing the prayer and action strategies that are essential for the sake of the harvest.

The league serves to unite these diverse teams around common kingdom goals while upholding a standard that reflects the character and values of the Bible. What are the requirements we ask of each person in this league? We ask them to **participate**, **communicate** and **cooperate**.

PARTICIPATION

To be effective and have strength of unity requires that every member of the league participates with the same understanding of what this entails. Participation means each church, ministry, or organization utilizes the 1Church1Day strategy for prayer and councils.

COMMUNICATION

When an army wants to defeat an enemy, their first action is to cut off the lines of communication. Communication is key to victory and includes components of supply and support. Members of the Kingdom League understand the high value of clear and regular communication with each other. This is accomplished by the use of the communication protocol utilized in the 1Church1Day strategy.

In scripture the Church is likened unto an army. Admirals and generals think and plan strategically. That means they have to plan supply and support to sustain their army in the field long term. Each league (city, region, etc.) will require a certain amount of financial honor to sustain long term strategic operations. The system encourages honor from the local church to the itinerant minister as each part does their share.

COOPERATION

We work together to achieve the same end. Kingdom League members know we are stronger together than we can ever be doing the same things separately, independent of one another. Cooperation in the league means to collaborate with the prayer and action strategies your league develops, and to follow the Golden Rule corporately. We want to see ministers lead their respective organizations to respond in prayer and action as they'd like to see the rest of the Church in their league cooperate with them.

NEXT STEPS

There are four different kinds of covenant relationship available through KLI.

- Family Members

- Tribe Members

- Fellow Workers

- Kingdom League

The **Family** or **Tribe Membership** is available for those who desire a close ministerial relationship. These offer the highest level of covenant and benefits such as providing a way to transition from a non-profit to a church, an association of churches and ministries, or an auxiliary of the church.

A **Fellow Worker** is anyone who shares our passion and desires to partner intentionally with our vision.

The **Kingdom League** is an association operating in an agreement which was established to accompany the 1Church1Day strategy. It helps local leaders establish their own league.

If you are interested in exploring any of these forms of covenant relationship, have questions, or you desire to learn more about transitioning from a non-profit to a church, please contact us using the information below and note your area of interest such as:

- Family or Tribe Membership

- 501(c)(3) verses a Church and an association of churches and ministries under 508(c)(1)(a).

- Partnering as a Fellow Worker

- Establishing a Kingdom League in your city or region

15

Leagues & The 1Church1Day Strategy

O ver the last two decades, I have pioneered a mobilization strategy called 1Church1Day (formerly called Operation Rolling Thunder or CONECT (Christian Outreach Network Establishing Church-wide Teamwork). This strategy has been used by leaders in over thirty-eight nations from Charismatic to Catholic and from Pentecostal to Presbyterian to unite the Church to build our Father's house of prayer for all nations, present Jesus' gospel of the kingdom, seat kingdom-minded leaders in the seven spheres of society, and to position the Church to make disciples. It's empowered leaders to mobilize the body of Christ as the army of the Lord. It is a powerful, diverse, strategic prayer army engaged in proclaiming God's word in their respective jurisdictions so as to release angelic forces to engage in spiritual battle.

I've discovered that the communities which enjoy long term transformation share seven common characteristics (see www.1Church1Day.org/results for examples). They are:

- **Honor God's Word**

- **Honor the gifts Christ gave**

- **Honor God's plans**

- **Have some sort of covenant agreement**

- **Honor jurisdictions**

- **Measure results and report**

- **Honor all people**

This strategy has proven to be cross-cultural and reproducible. Our system's design was driven by biblical mandate. In other words, we applied Matthew 6:9-12 and sought God's will and prioritized His desire over people's perceived needs. It positions leaders to do the same as they discover God's will for their respective communities. The application of God's wisdom is also included, and it empowers kingdom-minded leaders to mobilize the body of Christ as the army of the Lord to pray strategically for our Lord's kingdom to come and will be done.

Based upon our experience in mobilizing and connecting churches to transform their community, we've discovered that teamwork is essential. Therein lies the reason why we are using the proven concept of covenant to empower churches, cities, regions and states to form their own leagues.

THREE LEAGUES

The first is Kingdom League International. It's for those who desire to be directly connected to us as part of the KLI Family, Tribe or as a Fellow Worker described in the last chapter. These are those who ally together with us to continue pioneering new strategies and concepts that serve this generation to unite and mobilize the Church in these end times.

The next two kinds of leagues serve those who desire to utilize the 1Church1Day strategy to mobilize their network or community. These leagues help churches/ ministries serve their city, town or networks like leagues (football, basketball, baseball) serve cities who want to offer their sport and the ability to form and connect teams in their community and league.

The leagues provide a pattern which helps the teams connect at a greater level. The greater the level the higher and more skilful the play. It's like the difference between teams in a sand lot pick up game verses a college or Major League baseball team.

Kingdom League International is like that. We provide a pattern that helps another community or network form their own league. Motivated by Jesus prayer in John 17:21, we also provide a way for a city league to connect to a county league and a county league to a state league, etc.

Each network or community selects their leaders, their elders, their councils and determines the name of their league. They choose their prayer targets, establish their own metrics and use the 1Church1Day system to help them form their teams of churches and ministries who pray along with the teams of leaders from the seven spheres of society.

AN AMBASSADOR LEAGUE

The second league is called an Ambassador League. This is where everyone starts. It's made for the aspiring leader or network who desires to transform their community and establish continual prayer. This is called an Ambassador League because the leaders who start this league act as ambassadors for King Jesus who go to other churches, inviting them to pray and collaborate with the body of Christ in their territory. They are typically motivated by Jesus prayer in John 17:21 where Jesus prayed we'd be one and they are passionate about establishing 24/7/365 prayer all year long. Recognizing that prayer serves as a catalyst for revival and harvest they also seek to develop evangelistic strategies and see the value in establishing a strategic hub to coordinate the efforts of the Church in their community.

Ambassador Leagues begin to employ the 1Church1Day strategy using a little technology combined with our tried and true proven training, tools and systems. KLI's 1Church1Day app, available in the Google Play or the App Store in Apple, is offered in support of their efforts We use the 1Church1Day app combined with proven tools and training for Ambassador League leaders.

In 2017 the first Ambassador Leagues (India Prayer League, Transform Yakima Together League, the Snoqualmie Valley House of Prayer League, and the Sno-King Prayer League) were formed.

To learn how to start an Ambassador League visit www.kingdomleague.org/ambassador-league.

A KINGDOM LEAGUE

The third league is a Kingdom League. It's called a Kingdom League because we unite our church teams and leadership teams to pray and work together to present Jesus' gospel of the kingdom.

The primary difference between an Ambassador League and a Kingdom League is the networks maturity. As more churches, people, and leadership teams are added to pray and work together monthly the need for a strategic communication system becomes clear. A church or network transitions into a Kingdom League whenever they choose to utilize our technology to create their own strategic hub. It's a customized version of the 1Church1Day Community Transformation System. It includes a

Leadership Dashboard with their own mobile apps connecting the leaders and the people who pray together.

Communication is the key to increasing power through the power of agreement in prayer. Leviticus 26:8 says five will chase a 100 but a 100 will chase 10,000. Facilitating 24/7 prayer church by church and gleaning the wisdom as to what we the Church ought to pray and do from each council of leaders takes administration. It takes leadership. It is the mature networks with many congregations and ministries collaborating together who need a comprehensive communication system; a strategic command center so to speak.

Transform Yakima Together was made up of some of the leaders who began working with us as we pioneered this strategy in 2006 and 2007. In fact, their testimony regarding how prayer lowered crime by 50% is recorded in my book Operation Rolling Thunder. They started their Ambassador League in 2017 (Transform Yakima Together League). They had already been using this strategy in some fashion for over 10 years and they quickly decided that the tempo of ministry operations in the different spheres of society combined with the large volume of prayer would be served better by starting their own kingdom league.

The Transform Yakima Together League received their customized system in the first quarter of 2018.

Our system is designed for leaders who believe in our Lord's mandate to make disciples of all nations and who believe we are called to serve as kings and priests (Revelation 1:6 and 5:10). Kings make decrees and lead the charge in spiritual war (Revelation 19:11-14) while priests are called to intercede *(Hebrews 7:25)*. The app's dashboard consists of the following sections.

- **Decrees**—There are several categories in the Decree section based upon the leadership team each league forms. These leaders provide the prayer targets. As each church and person stands their watch, we encourage them to pray and proclaim the decrees here. This is one of the ways we leverage the prayer of agreement.

- **Alerts**—This section is used to send emergency prayer alerts or general information announcements.

- **Reports**—This section includes Watchman, Intercessor, Council, and Praise Report as well as Prayer Requests and a 1C1D Briefing. The more people pray, the more we expect them to see and hear and this provides a way for us to be good stewards of what God says.

- **Results**—This section tracks how many people, churches, days and hours of prayer have been mobilized, displays a map of the area being targeted and also has a section for testimonies.

- **Calendar**—This section includes calendars for Individuals, Churches, or Councils. This is where each person schedules their watch for each month and churches/ministries schedule their day of prayer.

- **Training**—This section provides end users all they need to know to use the app and each league can deploy their own videos or audio through this system as well.

A Leadership Dashboard serves as the hub that connects it all together. It's the strategic communication center or command center so to speak. This is where the real power is as all of the spiritual intelligence is gathered here and the "League Administrator" can prepare a brief, a consolidated report for the teams of leaders. Each of these councils can seek the Lord for counsel as well as apply Proverbs 24:3-6 which tells us that we develop plans to build and to war through wise counsel.

Psalm 68:11 says: "The Lord gave the word, and great was the company of those who proclaimed it." These councils of leaders help us determine the word of the Lord the Church is to pray and these are shared in the Decree or prayer Alert sections. This is how we leverage the power of agreement and is one of the strategic keys to the amazing results we see churches and networks producing around the world.

If you would like to learn more about what it takes to establish a Kingdom League for your church, community or network visit www.1church1day.org/leagues1.html.

WHAT IS THE COVENANT?

Each network, church or ministry who chooses to utilize this system adopts the league charter. It honors local spiritual authority and empowers them to lead using God's word. Each person who downloads an app agrees to abide by the covenant or league. We ask them to commit to:

- **Collaborate**—Each person agrees to stand watch at least one hour per month and each church or ministry agrees to cover one day with 24/7 prayer each month.

- **Communicate**—A reporting system is provided for those who pray to record anything they receive during their prayer time. Results are tracked, reported and adjustments are made to our decrees and prayer targets to make our efforts even more effective.

- **Cooperate**—Prayer decrees are created by strategic leaders from the 7 spheres of society. We encourage believers in each community to connect, support and pray as you co-labor together in Christ.

TO GOD BE THE GLORY

We understand that Christ called us to pioneer this strategic system. Our job is that of a son who seeks to serve and watch over that which our heavenly Father loves: His Church. The Church whom He sent His only begotten Son, our Lord Jesus Christ to shed His blood for. Therefore, this network of networks is not ours but rather His. The results and the glory all belong to our Lord.

I believe there is a new breed of leader that God has raised up for this time. Most are unknown and emerging. Their passionate love for our Lord will not allow them to touch the Church in an unholy manner. They see the Church like a bride being prepared for her Bridegroom.

I pray we hit the mark in this day. It is these kinds of leaders whom we are called to serve. If you believe this system and strategy can serve you and Christ's purpose in your congregation, community or network let us know. It would be an honor to serve you.

In His service,

**To learn more visit www.1Church1Day.org
and www.KingdomLeague.org.**

KINGDOM LEAGUE INTERNATIONAL

4004 NE 4ᵀᴴ ST.
SUITE 107-350
RENTON, WA 98056

WWW.KINGDOMLEAGUE.ORG

---

220 Auto pay

240 = 5.00   60
        GO B.

6824 - 18.00   37.92 credit

6892 - 31.08   37.92 "Credit
        18.00

160
180

Made in United States
Orlando, FL
10 April 2022

16694539R00059